It takes
courage
to be
who
you
truly are.

growing old is mandatory, growing up is optional.
Walt Disney

If you do
your best
each and every
day.
Good things
are sure
to
come your
way.

Let it go...

The flower that
blooms in adversity
is the most rare and beautiful of all.

Listen with your heart

Thank you for purchasing this book by the Chubby Mermaid/Deborah Muller

Please leave a review on Amazon.

Follow me on FB: Chubby Mermaid Art by Deborah Muller
Instagram: Chubby Mermaid Art
Website: ChubbymermaidArt.com
Etsy: Chubby Mermaid
Pinterest: Deborah Muller and Chubby Mermaid Art
Come join my colorng group on FB: Deborah Muller's Coloring Group

Made in the USA
San Bernardino, CA
01 August 2019